Sacred Economics: Expanding the Overton Window

a Sermon by

Rev. "Twinkle" Marie Manning

Matrika Press
a Sermon in My Pocket Series

Thought for Contemplation:

*"We're only haunted by the things we
refuse to accept."*

\- Bridgett Devoue

Dedication

For my children & grandchildren, and
For all seekers of The Beloved Community.

May we co-create Peace On Earth.

ISBN: 978-1-946088-70-3
Library of Congress:

1.Spirituality 2.Religion 3.Mindfullness
4.Interfaith 5.Economics 6.Nature
7.Peace 8.Prayer 9.Title

Matrika Press

*M*atrika *P*ress

www.MatrikaPress.com
www.TwinklesPlace.org
www.RSOTDE.org

ABOUT THIS BOOK SERIES

"a Sermon in My Pocket" series is
part of the "a Pocketful Book" collection
by Matrika Press.

This collection of pocket-sized books (4×6)
are ideal for poetry, meditations,
sermons or reflections, or
a collection of quotes and ideas.

This size is optimal for seasoned authors
wishing to offer a glimpse of their work
to readers in a pocket-size easy-to-carry edi-
tion. Also, this is an accessible first
endeavor for emerging authors
who desire to publish.

It is with delight we include in our
"a Sermon in My Pocket" series this
sermon by Rev. "Twinkle" Marie Manning
entitled, "Sacred Economics: Expanding the
Overton Window."

Her sermon was originally presented to the
Universalist Unitarian Church of Waterville,
Maine, USA.

Sacred Economics: Expanding the Overton Window

by Rev. "Twinkle" Marie Manning

This sermon's theme has been unpacked from first a paper file originally created in 2001 entitled, "Attaining World Peace."

In 2005 I transferred into my computer file. I changed the title over the years and added many subfiles - filling it ever since.

The file folders are replete with musings and research on:

- Environmental Stewardship Creating Safe Communities;

- Maintaining Intentional Life-styles;

- Merits & Practices of Intentional Communities;

- Conflict Negotiation;

- Democracy Distinctions;

- Paths to Achieving Accessible Healthcare for All
 ... *Not* "Affordable"
 ... Healthcare for All:
 Accessible!

- Healing Poverty and all its Accompanying impediments;

- Sourcing Renewable Energy Solutions;

- Sacred Economics;

and

- The Common Good.

These are a few of the subfiles with access to rabbit holes occupying years of hours.

All that to say that this is a topic I've thought about endlessly. It is in many ways what I envision as the Shambhala of social ecosystems.

I believe it will eradicate most of the suffering that exists on our planet today.

The premise is simple.

We each have gifts, talents. We donate them to the collective gift basket. In return we receive what we need. Everyone thrives.

Today I will give you the Cliff's Notes version :)

First - Some Definitions!

The Overton Window:

The Overton Window was designed in the 1990s by political scientist Joseph Overton.

It is meant to categorize the range of subjects and arguments politically acceptable to the mainstream population at a given time.

Imagine a window with a fixed frame; the sides of the window representing the furthest extremes of the political spectrum. They are outside this window.

Liberal to Conservative;
Left to Right.

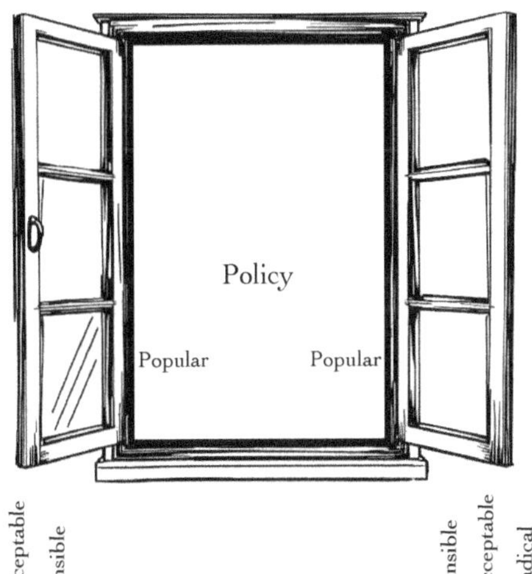

At the furthest reaches outside, gradually working inward, are ideas that fall into these categories:

- Unthinkable

- Radical

- Acceptable

As you get closer to the window

- Sensible appears.

Within the window frame - inside the window - on either side, close to the frame, is what is considered
- Popular

Left Popular. Right Popular. Liberal's Popular and Conservative's Popular. And in the very middle of is:
- Policy

Unthinkable: Are ideas just completely outside current societal norms. Many could be vile actions. Others could have been considered simply not possible. Such as Space Travel up until our century or so.

Radical: Are ideas sometimes considered dangerous (in reality or to disrupt status quo). But always considered fringe. We don't talk about these Radical Ideas in public. Not in anyway that would indicate that we supported them or believed in them. Belief in Aliens - visitors from other planets - would have been in this category just a few years ago.

Acceptable: Are ideas that are beginning to gain mainstream, they are showing up in discussions, and people are open to talking about them.

Sensible: Are ideas viewed as rational and reasonable policy alternatives. Now, sometimes they are exclusive to each side of the political aisle. What's "sensible" to someone who is Liberal may not quite be "sensible" to someone who is Conservative. What's "sensible" to someone who is Conservative may not be "sensible" to someone who is Liberal. But they can see that they are in the same window and they are part of public discourse.

Popular: Are ideas widely supported by the public. These popular ideas become Policy. It doesn't mean they are the "best" ideas. They become Policy largely dependent on who is in the lead - Liberal to Conservative - at any given time.

Policy: These are the ideas already enacted into law.

That's the Overton Window.

Next Definition...

Sacred Economics:

Charles Eisenstein, an American author, speaker, and activist known for exploring themes of environmentalism, alternative economics, and spirituality first coined the phrase "Sacred Economics" and describe the concept of "The Gift

Economy" in his 2011 book, Sacred Economics: Money, Gift, and Society in the Age of Transition.

While in large part his work is a critique of Capitalism. His goal of introducing the premise that realigns the monetary system to "sacred" values, such as natural, social, and spiritual capital, aiming to eliminate scarcity and foster reconnection between people and the environment.

He gives examples of how Capitalism destroys the environment by its very nature. For instance, if two people go to a bank seeking a loan to purchase a large parcel of land in the rain forest.

One person offers a presentation on how they strive to keep intact this beautiful ecosystem. They brought with them abundant information and offer examples of how the rainforest is essential for regulating the global climate, preserving biodiversity, and supporting human life. That these ecosystems act as critical carbon sinks, storing massive amounts of carbon dioxide and providing up to 23% of the climate mitigation needed to cool the planet. They regulate water cycles, prevent floods and droughts, and house over half of the world's species.

He would like the bank's help to save this land. But he offers no financial gain to the bank.

The other person's presentation is entirely focused on amassing wealth for their partners by destroying the land. She offers details on their investors that will match the loan if received. She shows their other bank statements and credit scores showing their ability to repay the loan, with interest, in the agreed upon time. She provides spreadsheets with the calculations supporting these claims.

In our current society, who receives the money from the bank?

In a Sacred Economy, the environment would be prioritized over profit. In fact, "profit" as we know it would eventually not exist.

Sacred Economics spans the entire realm of environmental focuses and social mechanisms. It dismantles greed and concentrates on The Common Good.

Now, my version of designing a Sacred Economy goes beyond Charles' description. Though, I think we ultimately get to a similar place.

He describes a slow integration of a new economic system. I would prefer to expedite the transition.

I think it is passed time we placed Sacred Economics in the Sensible and Popular sections of the Overton Window!

Or expand the window to include

ideas deemed Radical by those in power.

Third Definition...

Isocracy:

Iocracy is a system of government or a state where all citizens have equal political power. Deriving from Greek words for (isos) which means "equal" and (kratos) which means "power or rule."

Isocracy is equality of power.

The term was used in the mid-1600s, though is considered entirely theoretical. Discussions of Isocracy are typically limited to political philosophy and fiction.

Brief mentions of it have been found by poet Robert Southey (1796) and Rev. Sydney Smith (1845). Though - for transparency - neither of those two men supported the idea of "pure democratic equality."

Rev. Smith especially was opposed to it,

"If such 'Isocrats' were truly prepared to grant women the right to vote."

So, definitely a radical and dangerous idea!

Often when it does pop up in conversations, it is met with the query:

You mean anarchy?

No, not if you mean anarchy that begets chaos.

- Isocracy means equal power.

- No one ruling over another.

- No permanent hierarchy.

- No elite class deciding who deserves what.

- Decisions are made collectively.

- Leadership roles rotate.

- Transparency is the norm.

- Isocracy doesn't eliminate responsibility.

- It distributes it.

- And when power is shared, exploitation loses its hiding places.

I believe it is time to place Isocracy in the Overton Window's public conversation portals. For Sacred Economics cannot function inside systems of domination.

We are living in an era of unbelievable contradiction.

- We produce enough food to feed everyone — yet people are hungry.

- We build more homes than ever before — yet people are unhoused.

- We possess medical knowledge that could prevent immense suffering — yet people do suffer everyday and even die because they cannot afford care.

So the problem is not scarcity.

The problem is the story we are living inside. And it desperately needs to shift.

The ideals I present as sacred economics are:

Not as utopia.

Not as mere theory.

But as a practical, compassionate response to the suffering we see every day.

Sacred Economics as offered by Charles Eisenstein traces the history of money from ancient gift economies to modern capitalism, revealing how the money system has contributed to alienation, competition, and scarcity, destroyed community, and necessitated endless growth.

Growth as primary method; and Profit as Holy Grail.

Charles points out that:

"Money has become an end in itself, rather than a means to an end."

Regardless the harm caused to planet and people. Because when money becomes the end, life becomes negotiable.

Sacred Economics introduces the realization that Money is not just a tool.

It is a story about who matters.

The world we live in measures poverty by income, not by outcome, certainly not by access.

When money becomes the medium through which all needs must pass, human life is sorted into categories:

Worthy.
Unworthy.
Insured.
Uninsured.
Housed.
Unhoused.
Citizen.
Noncitizen.

Sacred Economics asks us to change the central question of society.

Instead of asking,
  "Can you pay?"
We ask,
  "What do you need to live well?"

And then — this is the radical part — we organize ourselves to meet those needs directly.

And we do so in every aspect of our lives!

Because these conversations create a certain level of cognitive dissonance as they are shifting the narrative and focus completely from what our mind's perceive as always ever been, sometimes it is best to begin with one of the predominant edifices of Capitalism - or perhaps a quick definition of Capitalism is in order:

Capitalism: is an economic and political system in which private individuals and companies own the "means of production" (like factories, land, and resources) and operate them for profit, with prices and production driven by competition and supply & demand in a free market, rather than by government control.

Some argue that Capitalism, through innovation, generates wealth and reduces poverty - at least when compared to some systems. While others contend it inherently creates poverty through inequality, exploitation, and skewed wealth distribution.

Proponents argue that a pursuit of excellence is a natural, emergent outcome of the capitalist system, yet critics see it as a pursuit solely of profit that most often bypasses higher virtues and excellence.

Thereby markets are flooded with mediocre, subpar, low quality products as owners and investors strive to make the most profit rather than striving to make the best products and services.

In a society shaped around Sacred Economics every industry would thrive in the pursuit of excellence!

Manufacturing's hallmark would be Collaboration Over Competition.

As a result, the Earth and All Her Residents would Benefit!

Today's industries compete relentlessly — producing waste, planned obsolescence, and environmental harm.

In a sacred economic system:

- Industries collaborate.

- Knowledge is shared.

- Redundancy is reduced.

- Products are designed to last.

Isn't it ironic that it is commonplace to have "warrantees" on products, like cars and electronics, that expire timed exactly when their components break down?

When excellence and not profit as the goal, and with values of environmental sustainability, we would begin to see products that last many lifetimes.

And, the thing is - the technology to do so already exists. It is throttled to align with the goal of profit.

It's time to change the question of:
"How do we sell more?"

To:
"How do we serve life better?"

When we do, innovation flourishes—not from profit pressure, but from purpose aligned with values.

The same is true across the board!

Beginning with Our Earth!

We see Earth as Sacred, not as Commodity.

Our current economy rewards destruction.

You can poison water and still be successful.

Strip forests and be celebrat-
ed.

Sacred Economics changes the incentive structure entirely.

When there is no profit in harm, the Earth is no longer a resource.

She is someone we are in relationship with.

Cleanup happens because it must.

Restoration becomes meaningful work.

Regeneration replaces exploitation.

Caring for the planet is no longer a side project or worthy cause. It is central to collective well-being.

Healthcare:

In our current system, illness is terrifying not only because of pain— but because of cost.

A diagnosis can mean debt.

Treatment can mean bank-
ruptcy.

And, that is if you can access
healthcare at all.

In a sacred economic system:

Healthcare is not a commodity.
It is a collective promise.

*Healthcare is not a commodity.
It is a collective promise!*

When someone is sick, the question is not,
"How will you pay?"

The question is,
"How can we help?"

Doctors, nurses, therapists, caregivers offer their skills as part of the shared well-being of the community. And in return, their needs are met — housing, food, rest, care.

Access to medications becomes simple.

Direct. Human.

No insurance labyrinth.

No profit-driven scarcity.

No one choosing between medicine and survival.

Preventive care becomes the norm.

Mental health support becomes accessible.

People receive help early — before suffering multiplies.

Housing:

How about We End the Crisis That Never Should Have Existed!

There is no housing shortage.
There is no housing shortage!
There is a moral shortage.

More and more homes are treated as investments, not as places where human life unfolds.

In a sacred economic system:
Everyone has a safe place to live.

Not someday.

Not after proving worth on a spreadsheet.

Now!

Homes are allocated based on need — family size, accessibility, location. *And, they can be as beautiful as we want them to be!*

Maintenance is collective.

Repairs are timely.

Environmental hazards are not ignored.

Mold is cleaned.

Lead is removed.

Unsafe conditions are addressed immediately.

Future planning takes all this and more into consideration.

And, in a crisis:
If a pipe freezes and bursts in wintertime, or if there is damage

from a storm - it is repaired as quickly as possible.

Buildings are not bought as part of a depreciating portfolio - left vacant or empty and seeking tax credit as a "loss."

Why?

Because when no one profits from neglect, care becomes common sense.

Housing becomes what it was always meant to be - a foundation for dignity.

Likewise with Food!

Everyone in this envisioned society has plenty of nutritious food to eat.

The Earth provides bountifully.

In a Sacred Economy it is shared.

Access to it is no longer denied on bases of financial merit.

Access.

Dignity.

Safety.

Freedom.

These permeate throughout a Sacred Economy.

One of the most profound impacts of eliminating money is the freedom it creates — especially for up until now at risk populations and, among them, women.

Financial dependence traps countless women in unsafe homes and violent relationships.

Money becomes leverage.

Survival becomes a threat.

In a Sacred Economic society, no one is financially trapped.

Not by circumstance.

Not by divorce.

Not by how many children they have.

Housing, food, healthcare, and community support are guaranteed.

Leaving an unsafe situation does not mean poverty, homelessness, or isolation.

When we remove systems that pit survival against safety, we allow people—especially women and those at risk—to choose life, dignity, and peace.

This is not abstract freedom.

This is embodied freedom.

The new norm becomes Collaboration not Domination.

Those accustomed to demonstrating the latter — *domination* — will become inclined to adopt peaceableness and nonviolence as it is the Only Acceptable way of being.

A Sacred Economy Means The End of Exploitation and Trafficking!

Human trafficking exists because it is profitable.

Forced labor exists because it generates money.

Remove the money — and the engine collapses.

In a system without buying and selling human beings:

There is nothing to exploit for gain.

Nothing to traffic.

Nothing to hoard.

And, in a society that operates within the framework of an Isocracy, there is no elite class quietly benefiting from harm.

Communities are organized
to notice.

To intervene.

To protect.

Care replaces coercion.

Transparency
replaces secrecy.

Happiness, Meaning, and Time

When having our basic needs met is guaranteed, people change.

They choose work aligned with their gifts.

They rest without guilt.

They create without fear.

Our lives become more relaxed.

Time opens up.

For friendships.

For art.

For spiritual practice.

Mary Oliver asks us with her iconic question:
"Tell me, what is it you plan to do with your one wild and precious life?"

Sacred Economics makes it possible to answer that question honestly — and radically — without fear of starvation, eviction, or abandonment.

People are happier not because life is perfect - *I can't promise you perfection.*

But, people are happier because Life makes sense!

A World Without Power Over

At its heart, this vision is about trust. Trust that when artificial scarcity *(artificial scarcity!)* is removed, human beings do not become monsters, or lazy or selfish.

They become neighbors.

Stewards.

Caretakers.

Sacred Economics removes the question,
"What can I afford?"

Isocracy removes the question, *"Who is in charge?"*

And, that **Overton Window** is Wide Open with Possibilities!

Because, what remains is one of the oldest questions of all:

"How shall we care for one another and for the Earth that holds us?"

Some think I am naïve to think this. Let alone say it out loud — first in front of a microphone and audience — and now in this book!

But I believe it is incumbent on us to have radical conversations that do not just keep sliding the window slightly back and forth, relegating policy-making to benefit who currently holds power on a Red or Blue scale.

I don't believe it's naïve to point out the obvious:

This system is Not Working!

It is harming too many people.

It wreaking havoc on our planet.

It is necessary to shape another way.

And it is already being born!

Wherever people choose
- cooperation over competition,
- care over control,
and love over fear.

The time is now.

May it Be So.

Discussing Sacred Economics: Expanding the Overton Window

Key Words and Phrases:
The Overton Window
Sacred Economics
Gift Society
Isocracy
Capitalism
Planned Obsolescence
Exploitation
Cooperation

Talking Points:

1. Looking at the Overton Window pictured on page 11, list several ideas that are in each of the following categories:

- Unthinkable
- Radical
- Acceptable
- Sensible
- Popular
- Policy

2. What ideas that are currently considered "Radical" would you like to see placed in The Overton Window?

3. (a) What safeguards could be put in place to assure Isocracy is not corrupted?

   (b) How would you envision the most efficient government structure in an Isocracy? ie: What important roles would ideally be in place so that communities are served seamlessly.

   (c) Assuming leadership roles would rotate, what are ideal term-limits?

4. When planned obsolescence is eliminated and care for Earth and all its residents are the priority:

   (a) Which harmful aspects of our current system will be the easiest to remedy?

   (b) What best-practices will benefit manufacturing and fuel industries to able to swiftly adapt?

   (c) How do you envision the streamlining of infrastructure in regards to community planning, including food distribution, access to housing, medical care?

5. When people no longer need to "earn a living"

    (a) What job or creative endeavor do you hope to dedicate your time to?

    (b) What kinds of jobs do you envision will be a shared responsibility?

    (c) What aspects of the current system do you believe will be the most challenging for people in power, or even people with relative privilege, be most resistant to change?

6. Describe how a Sacred Economy or Gift Society could be ushered in peacefully.

Rev. Dr. "Twinkle" Marie Manning, D.D. is an ordained interfaith minister, retreat leader, poet and liturgist. She received her Doctor of Divinity, D.D. through the University of Sedona and is a member of the International Metaphysical Ministry. Twinkle strives to include many philosophies in her service. Her ministry often focuses on the earth-centered, esoteric, spiritually connected, community building and social justice aspects of her faith.

One of her ministry's core teachings is that of
Living Life As A Prayer.

Twinkle is a multi-disciplinary artist. She a published author and poet, intuitive acrylic and watercolor painter, mystical sketch-artist utilizing pencil, ink and charcoal, with additional creations spanning video, audio and digital media.

She is an award-winning television producer and podcast host. She is a former radio talk show host, columnist and luxury lifestyle magazine editor. She is an experienced public speaker, retreat leader and interfaith minister.

While most her published work is inspirational non-fiction and poetry, Twinkle has recently published her first children's book and is about to publish her first young adult and contemporary adult trade fiction novels.

Her poetry and writings
have been included in
spiritual rituals, funerals,
memorials, wedding
ceremonies, blessingways,
and coming-of-age gath-
erings in many locations
around the world.

Common themes of her ministry and writings
include:

Building The Beloved Community,

Curating Peace on Earth,

Embodying Compassion

Creating Spiritual Practices
that Honor the Earth and the Human Experience

For more information about Twinkle, visit:
www.TwinklesPlace.org

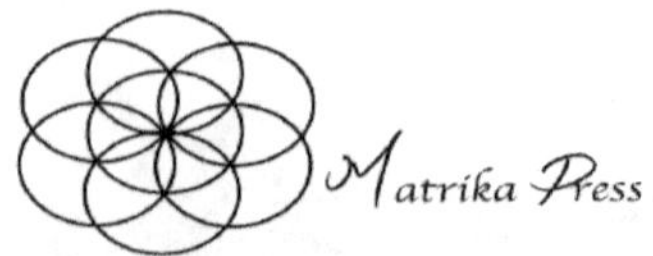

Matrika Press is an independent publishing house dedicated to publishing works in alignment with transformational religious and spiritual values and principles. Its fiscal sponsor is UU Women and Religion (www.uuwr.org) and Melusine's Haven (www.MelusinesHaven.org).

Matrika derives its name from the 50 letters of the Sanskrit alphabet called "the mothers" aka "Matrika." Kali Ma used the letters to form words, and from the words formed all things...as with the Bible: *"in the beginning was the Word."*

People of all backgrounds and faiths agree:
Words are powerful.
More than that: *Their vibrations are creative forces;*
they bring all things into being.

Matrika Press is part of the ministry of Rev. "Twinkle" Marie Manning and part of the larger nonprofit church known as Twinkle's Place, also known as RSOTDE. Matrika Press, along with TV for Your Soul, serve as the creative branch of the ministry's media projects. Matrika Press publishes anthologies, memoirs, poetry, prayer and ritual manuscripts, and other books to bring transformation to the world.

www.MatrikaPress.com

FIND OUT HOW
YOUR CONGREGATION OR GROUP *CAN HOST*
a local UU Talks in your community. UU Talks is a
speakers series, similar to TED Talks, where Speakers
will speak about topics aligned with UU Values.
Join Us!
www.UUTalks.org

*Above pictured: Inaugural UU Talks event
at the UUA Boston, 2017
Peter Bowden, Matt Meyer, Lydia Edwards, Rev. Allison Palm,
Jim Tull, Anna Huckabee Tull, Regie Gibson, Marlon Carey,
Rev. Hank Pierce, Rev. "Twinkle" Marie Manning*

OTHER TITLES BY THIS AUTHOR

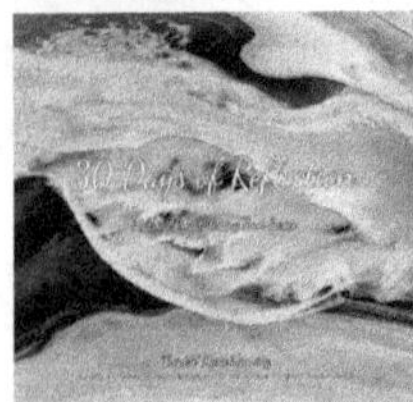

www.MatrikaPress.com

Cardinal Magic is the first book in the
Mora Mulberry series about a little girl who lives
by the ocean on a farm in Maine with her mother.
Mora and her friends are so happy to share their
adventures and lessons with you! This book is
about kindness and welcoming new friends. It also
offers strategies to help overcome stress.

www.MoraMulberry.com

GODDESS GUARDIAN
ORACLE CARDS

Designed by: "Twinkle" Marie Manning

Published by
MATRIKA PRESS

www.TwinklesPlace.org/GoddessCards

Empowering
W O M E N
Salon Gatherings
&
Signature Events

"Twinkle" Marie Manning
is the founder of the
Empowering Women TV project.
She and her friends host these amazing
gatherings! If you would like to attend,
or *Host one,*
in your community, visit:

www.EmpoweringWomenTV.org

Twinkle's Place

RETREAT CENTER & ARTIST RESIDENCY
www.TwinklesPlace.org

www.365DaysOfPoetry.com

Sacred Economics:
Expanding the Overton Window
a Sermon in My Pocket Series
by Matrika Press

This sermon addresses in clear terms the undeniable brokenness of our economic, social and environmental systems. It details the profound shift that needs to take place for the common good.

It offers a radical alternative that eradicates poverty, homelessness, and exploitation, even as it ushers in sustainability, justice and peace.

Join **Rev. "Twinkle" Marie Manning** as she explores a resetting of society through a foundation of sacred economics within the framework an isocracy.

*The path to a sacred economy
begins by expanding the Overton Window.*